Beautiful
The Carole King Musical

Front cover photo by Joan Marcus

ISBN 978-1-4950-8577-2

7777 W. BLUEMOUND RD. P.O. BOX 13819 MILWAUKEE, WI 53213

In Australia Contact:
Hal Leonard Australia Pty. Ltd.
4 Lentara Court
Cheltenham, Victoria, 3192 Australia
Email: ausadmin@halleonard.com.au

Visit Hal Leonard Online at
www.halleonard.com

Be-Bop-A-Lula

Words and Music by Tex Davis and Gene Vincent

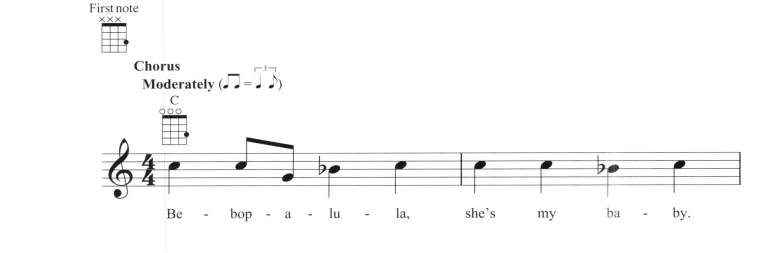

Be - bop - a - lu - la, she's my ba - by.

Be - bop - a - lu - la, I don't mean may - be. Be - bop - a - lu - la,

she's my ba - by. Be - bop - a - lu - la, I don't mean may - be.

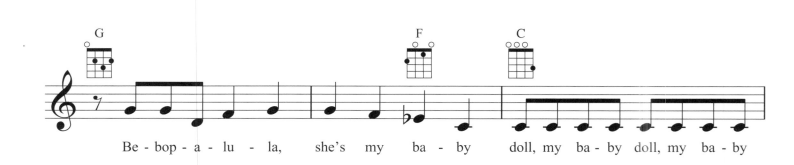

Be - bop - a - lu - la, she's my ba - by doll, my ba - by doll, my ba - by

Happy Days Are Here Again

Words and Music by Jack Yellen and Milton Ager

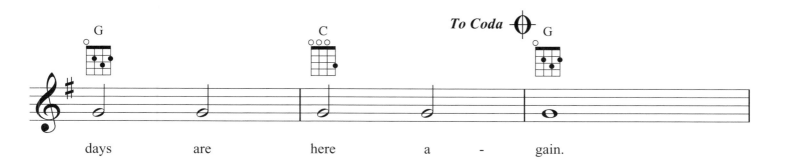

days   are   here   a -   gain.

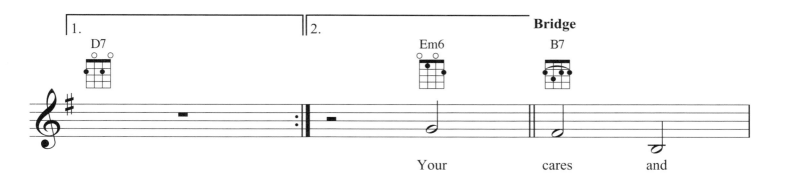

Your   cares   and

trou -   bles   are   gone.   There'll

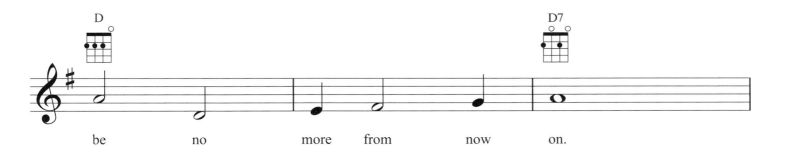

be   no   more   from   now   on.

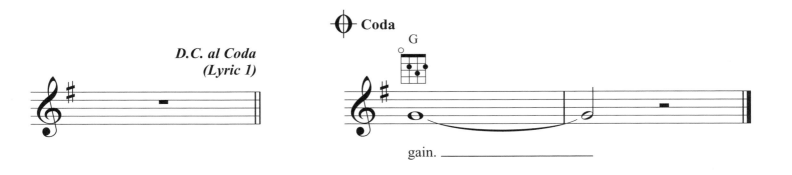

gain. _____

7

He's Sure the Boy I Love

Words and Music by Barry Mann and Cynthia Weil

First note

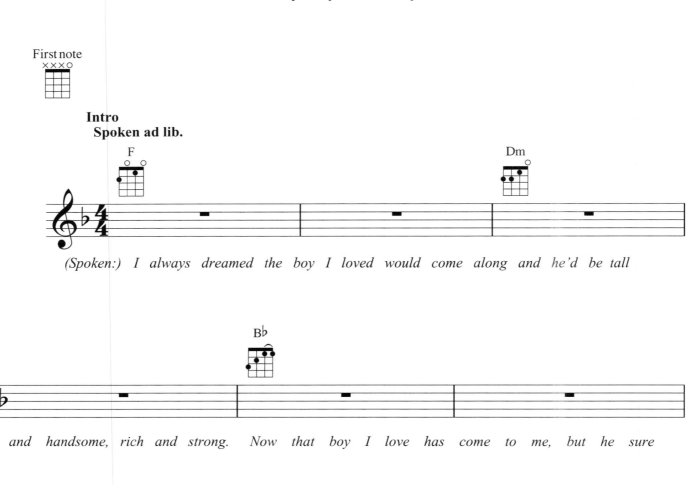

Intro
Spoken ad lib.

(Spoken:) I always dreamed the boy I loved would come along and he'd be tall

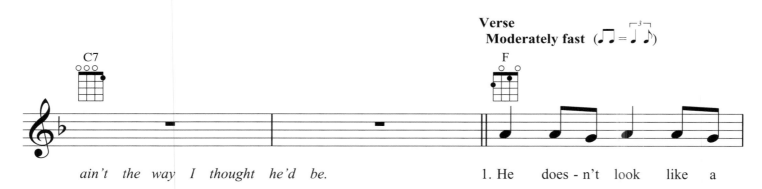

and handsome, rich and strong. Now that boy I love has come to me, but he sure

Verse
Moderately fast

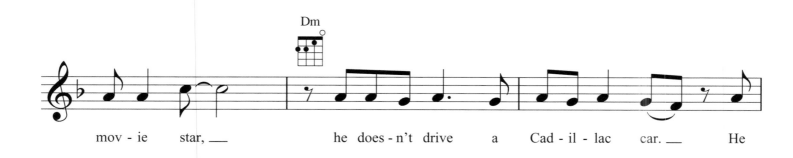

ain't the way I thought he'd be.   1. He does-n't look like a

mov-ie star, ___   he does-n't drive a Cad-il-lac car. ___   He

sure ain't the boy I've been dream-in' of, _____ but he's sure the boy I love. _

_____ Let me tell ya, now. 2. He'll nev - er be a big

bus' - ness man, _____ he al - ways buys on the in -

stall - ment plan. _____ He sure ain't the boy I've been

dream - in' of, _____ but he's sure the boy I love. _

Bridge

_____ 'Cause when he holds me tight, _____ ev - 'ry - thing's right, _____

cra - zy as it seems. ___ I'm his, what -

ev - er he is, ___ and I for - get all of my

Outro-Verse

dreams. Now ev - 'ry - bod - y knows that he does - n't hang dia - monds

'round my neck ___ and all he's got's an un - em -

ploy - ment check. ___ He sure ain't the boy I've been

dream - in' of, ___ but he's sure the boy I love. ___

Beautiful

Words and Music by Carole King

First note

You've got to get up ev - 'ry morn - in' ____ with a

smile on your face ____ and show the world ____ all the love ____ in your

heart. Then peo - ple gon - na treat you bet -

To Coda ⊕

- ter. ____ You're gon - na find, yes, ____ you will, ____ that you're beau -

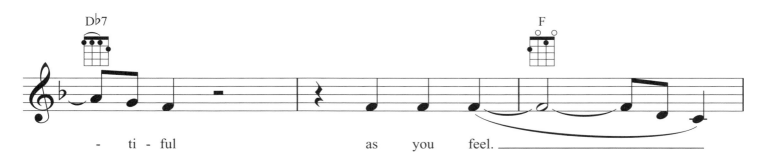

- ti - ful as you feel. ____

Verse

1. Wait - ing at the sta - tion with a work - day wind a - blow -
2. *See additional lyrics*

- ing, I've got noth - ing to do ____ but watch ____ the

pass - ers - by. _____ Mir - rored in their

fac - es I see frus - tra - tion grow - ing, and they

2nd time, D.C. al Coda

don't see it show - ing. Why ___ do I?

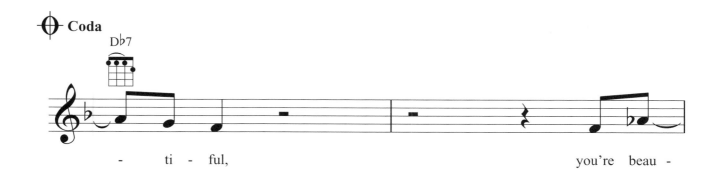

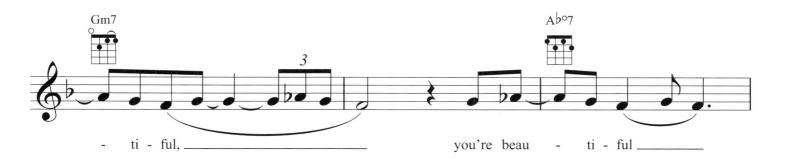

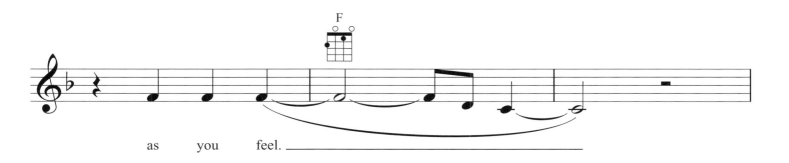

Additional Lyrics

2. I have often asked myself the reason for the sadness
   In a world where tears are just a lullaby.
   If there's any answer, maybe love can end the madness.
   Maybe not, oh, but we can only try.

I Feel the Earth Move

Words and Music by Carole King

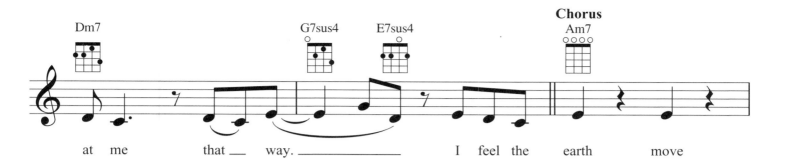

at me   that ___ way. _____   I feel the   earth   move

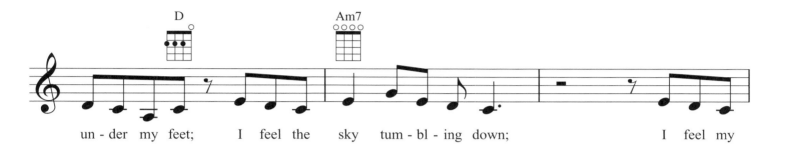

un - der   my feet;   I feel   the   sky   tum - bl - ing down;   I feel my

heart start to trem - bl - in'   when - ev - er ____ you're a - round. _____

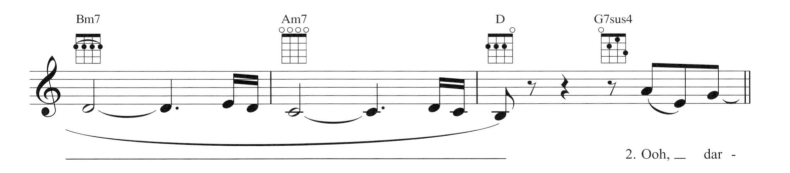

_____   2. Ooh, __ dar -

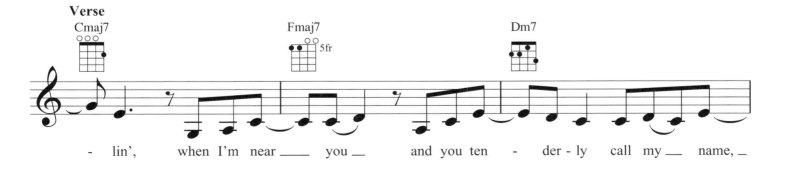

- lin',   when I'm near ____ you __   and you ten - der - ly call my __ name, __

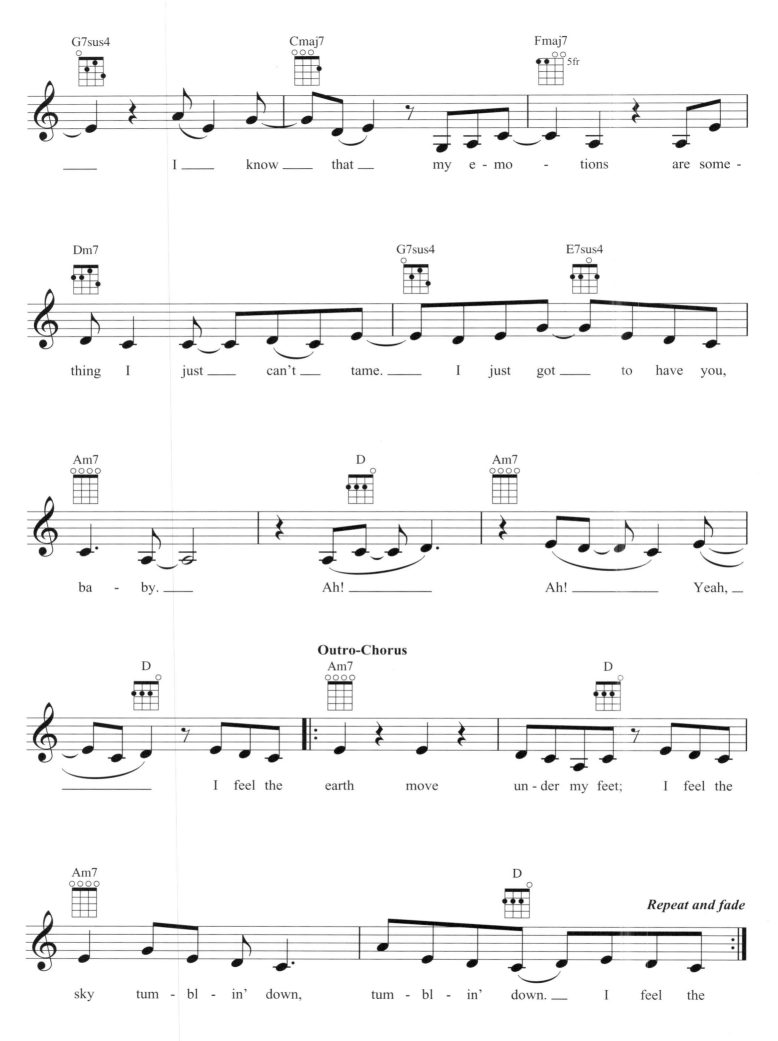

Chains

Words and Music by Gerry Goffin and Carole King

First note

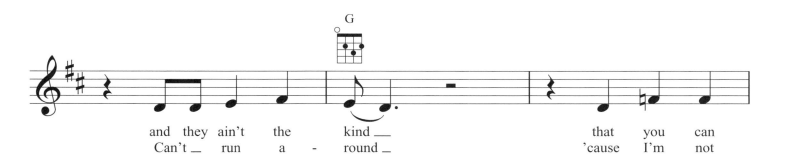

Chains, my ba-by's got me locked up in chains, __
Chains, well, I can't break a - way from these chains. __

and they ain't the kind __ that you can
Can't __ run a - round __ 'cause I'm not

see. _____ Whoa, __ these chains of love _____
free. _____ Whoa, __ these chains of love _____

1.

__ got a hold on me, __ yeah. __
__ won't let me be, __ yeah. __

1. Now, be-lieve me when I _____ tell ___ you
2. I wan-na tell you now, _____ ba - by,

that I think ___ you're fine. _____ I'd like to
your lips ___ look sweet. _____ I'd like to

love ___ you, ___ but, dar-ling, I'm im - pris-oned by these
kiss ___ them, ___ but I can't break a - way from all these

Chorus

chains. }
chains. }
My ba-by's got me locked up in chains, ___

and they ain't the kind ___ that you can

see. _____   Whoa, ___ these   chains   of   love _____

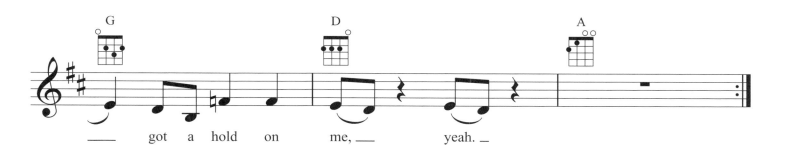

___   got   a   hold   on   me, ___   yeah. __

Outro

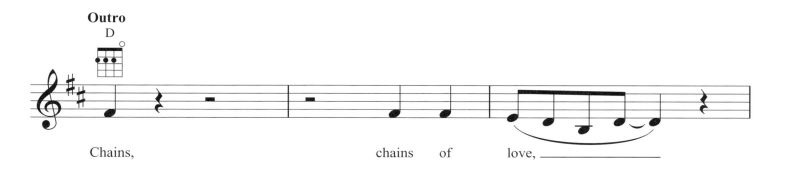

Chains,   chains   of   love, _____

chains   of   love, _____   chains   of

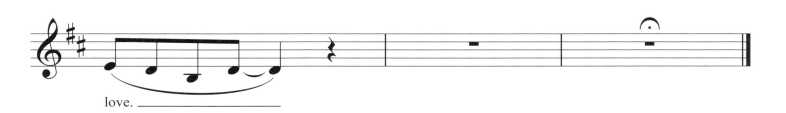

love. _____

It Might as Well Rain Until September

Words and Music by Gerry Goffin and Carole King

might as well   rain un - til Sep - tem - ber.
might as well   rain un - til Sep -
might as well   rain un - til Sep -

tem - ber.   My friends look   for - ward to their

pic - nics on the beach.   Yes, ev - 'ry - bod - y   loves the sum - mer -

time.   But you know, dar - ling, while your

arms are out of reach,   the sum - mer is - n't   an - y friend of

mine. _____

tem - ber.

It's Too Late

Words and Music by Carole King and Toni Stern

Additional Lyrics

2. It used to be easy living here with you.
   You were light and breezy and I knew just what to do.
   Now you look so unhappy, and I feel like a fool.

3. There'll be good times again for me and you.
   But we just can't stay together, don't you feel it, too?
   Still, I'm glad for what we had and how I once loved you.

(You Make Me Feel Like)
A Natural Woman

Words and Music by Gerry Goffin, Carole King and Jerry Wexler

kind.   Your   love   was   the   key   to   my   peace   of

for.   'Cause if   I   make you hap - py,   I don't need to do

Chorus

mind. ____ }   'Cause you make me ___ feel, _____   you make me ___

more. ____ }

feel, _____   you make me ___ feel like a ___ nat - u - ral

Bridge

wom - an.   Oh, ___ ba - by, what you've

done to me! ___ (What you've done to me!) ___   You ___ make me

feel ___ so ___ good _____ in - side.   (Good in - side.) ___

The Loco-Motion

Words and Music by Gerry Goffin and Carole King

First note

Verse
Moderately fast

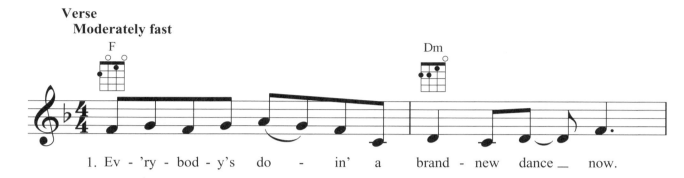

1. Ev - 'ry - bod - y's do - in' a brand - new dance __ now.

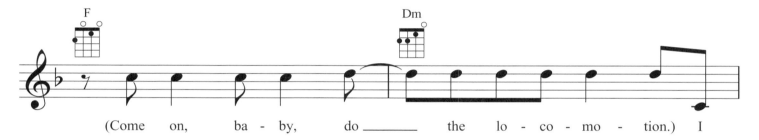

(Come on, ba - by, do __ the lo - co - mo - tion.) I

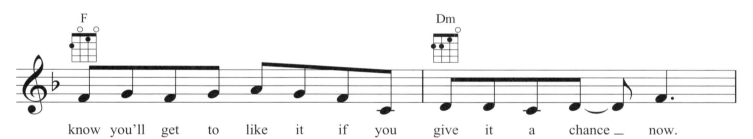

know you'll get to like it if you give it a chance __ now.

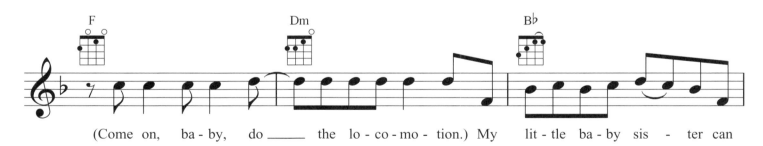

(Come on, ba - by, do __ the lo - co - mo - tion.) My lit - tle ba - by sis - ter can

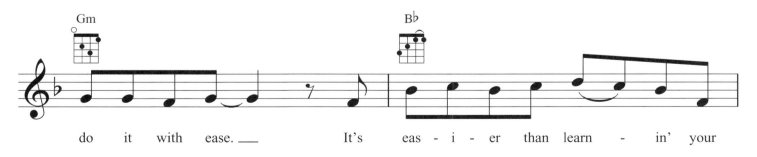

do it with ease. __ It's eas - i - er than learn - in' your

A - B - C's. ___ So come on, come on, do ___ the lo - co - mo - tion with

Bridge

me. You got - ta swing your hips now. Come on,

ba - by, jump up, ___ jump back. ___ Oh, well, I

Verse

think you got the knack. 2. Now that you can do ___ it,
3. Move a - round the floor ___ in a

let's make a chain ___ now. }
lo - co - mo - tion. }

(Come on, ba - by, do ___

___ the lo - co - mo - tion.) {A chug - a chug - a mo - tion like a
Do it hold - in' hands ___ if

Oh! Carol

Words and Music by Howard Greenfield and Neil Sedaka

On Broadway

Words and Music by Barry Mann, Cynthia Weil, Mike Stoller and Jerry Leiber

Additional Lyrics

2. They say the women treat you fine on Broadway.
   But lookin' at them just gives me the blues.
   'Cause how ya gonna make some time,
   When all you got is one thin dime?
   And one thin dime won't even shine your shoes.

3. They say that I won't last too long on Broadway.
   I'll catch a Greyhound bus for home, they say.
   But they're dead wrong, I know they are,
   'Cause I can play this here guitar.
   And I won't quit till I'm a star on Broadway.

One Fine Day

Words and Music by Gerry Goffin and Carole King

girl. *(Instrumental)*

Bridge

Though __ I know you're __ the kind ___ of boy _____

who on-ly ___ wants to run a-round, I'll ___ keep

wait-ting, ___ and some-day, dar-ling, ___

D.C. al Coda

you'll come to me when you want to set-tle down, oh.

Additional Lyrics

2. The arms I long for
   Will open wide,
   And you'll be proud to have me
   Walking by your side.

3. One fine day
   We'll meet once more,
   And then you'll want the love you
   Threw away before.

So Far Away

Words and Music by Carole King

do me ___ good. ___ How I wish ___ I could, but you're so

far a - way!

§ Verse

One more song a - bout mov - in' a - long ___ the high - way,
Trav - el - in' a - round sure gets ___ me down ___ and lone - ly.

can't say much of an - y - thing ___ that's new. If
Noth - in' else to do but close ___ my mind. I

I could on - ly work this life out ___ my ___ way, ___ I'd
sure ___ hope ___ the road don't come to own ___ me. ___ There's

rath - er spend ___ it ___ be - in' close to you, ___
so man - y ___ dreams ___ I've yet to find, ___ } but you're so

Pleasant Valley Sunday

Words and Music by Gerry Goffin and Carole King

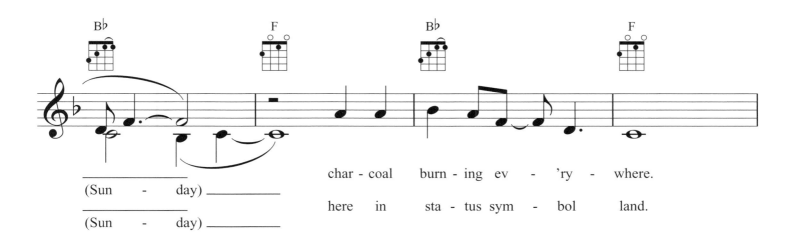

(Sun - day) _____

(Sun - day) _____

char - coal burn - ing ev - 'ry - where.

here in sta - tus sym - bol land.

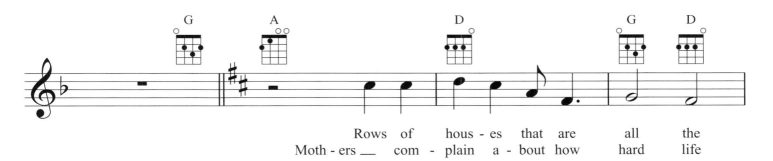

Rows of hous - es that are all the

Moth - ers ___ com - plain a - bout how hard life

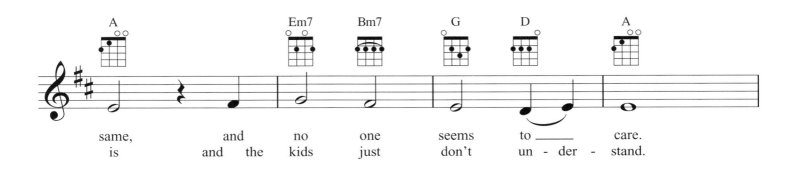

same, and no one seems to ___ care.

is and the kids one just don't un - der - stand.

1. 2. **Bridge**

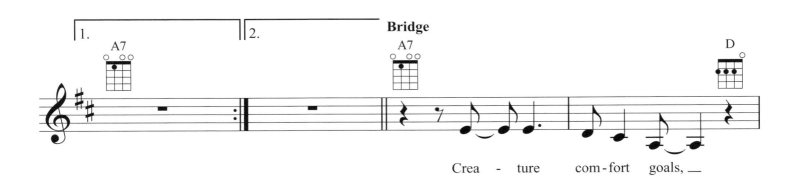

Crea - ture com - fort goals, ___

they on - ly numb ___ my soul and make it hard ___

for me to see. _____ My _____ thoughts all

seem to stray _____ to _____ plac - es _____ far a - way. _____

I need a change _____ of sce - ner - y. _____

Interlude

Verse

3. Ta ta ta ta _____ ta ta ta ta _____ ta ta ta ta _____

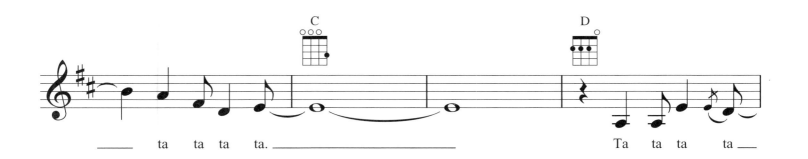

ta ta ta ta. Ta ta ta ta

ta ta ta ta ta ta ta ta ta ta ta.

Chorus

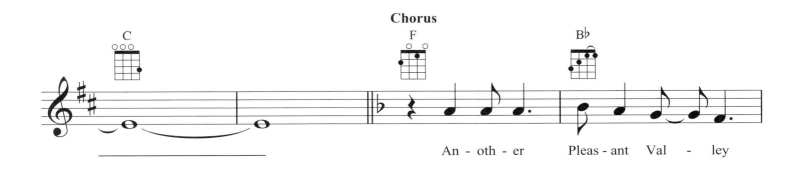

An - oth - er Pleas - ant Val - ley

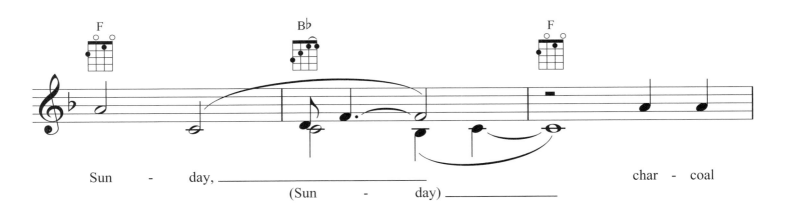

Sun - day, char - coal
(Sun - day)

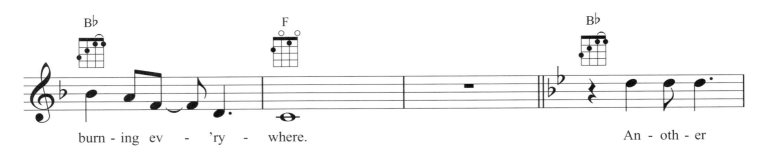

burn - ing ev - 'ry - where. An - oth - er

Outro

Repeat and fade

Some Kind of Wonderful

Words and Music by Gerry Goffin and Carole King

Bridge

won - der - ful!   I know I   can't __ ex - press

this feel - ing of   ten - der - ness. __   There's so __ much I __

want __ to   say, __   but the   right words just   don't __

come my   way. __   3. I   just know when   I'm in __

Verse

your em - brace   this world __ is a   hap - py place,

and __ some - thing   hap - pens to me   that's some kind of

46

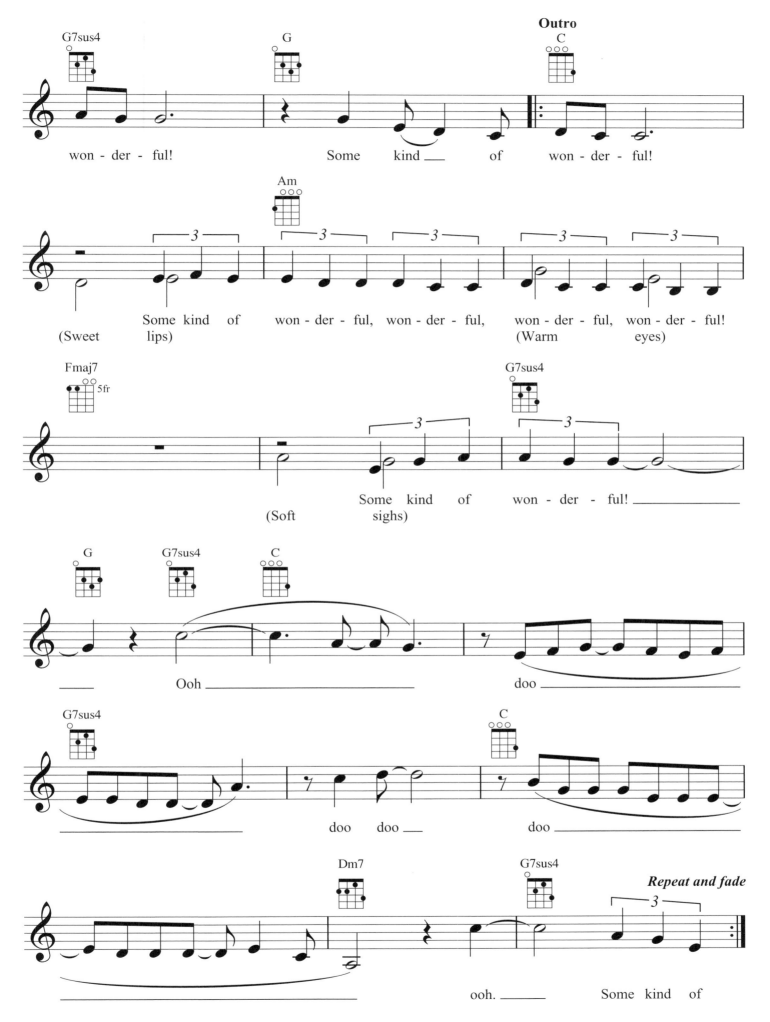

Outro

won - der - ful!   Some   kind ___ of   won - der - ful!   Some kind of   won - der - ful, won - der - ful,   won - der - ful, won - der - ful!

(Sweet   lips)   (Warm   eyes)

Some   kind   of   won - der - ful! _____

(Soft   sighs)

Ooh _____   doo _____

_____ doo doo ___   doo _____

Repeat and fade

ooh. _____   Some kind of

47

Take Good Care of My Baby

Words and Music by Gerry Goffin and Carole King

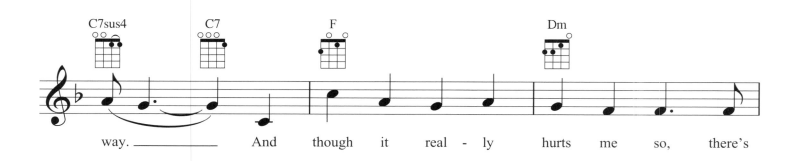

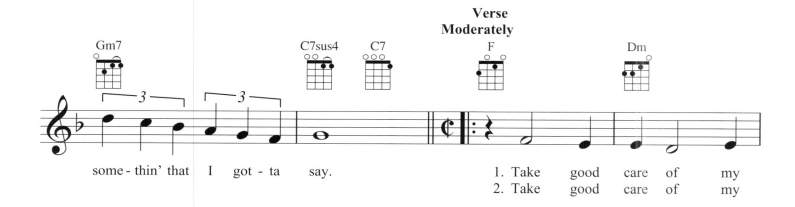

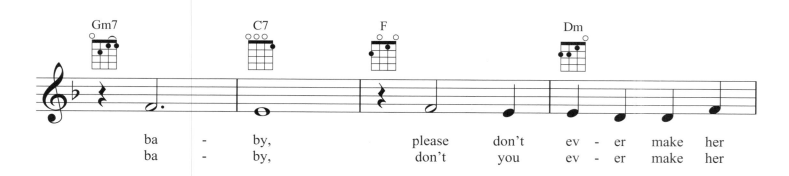

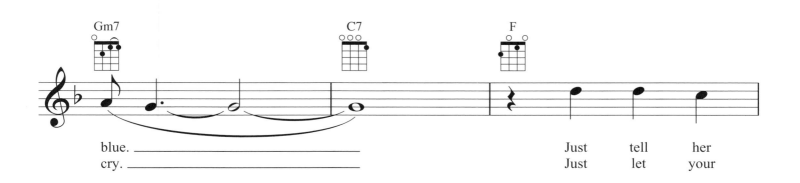

blue. _____ Just   tell   her
cry. _____ Just   let   her   your

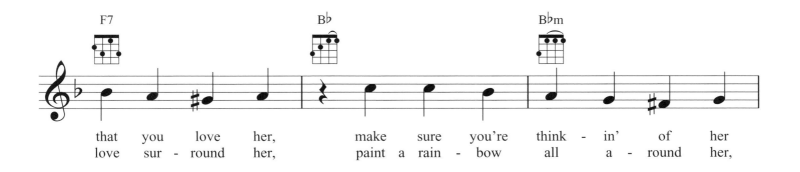

that   you   love   her,   make   sure   you're   think - in'   of   her
love   sur - round   her,   paint   a   rain - bow   all   a - round   her,

1.
in   ev - 'ry - thing   you   say   and   do. _____
don't   let   her

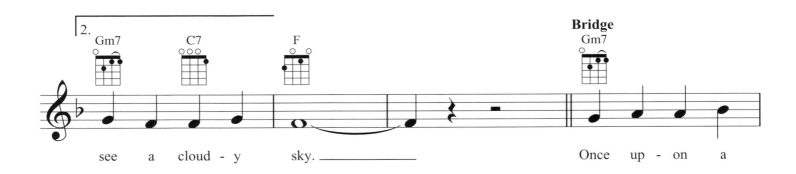

2.
Bridge
see   a   cloud - y   sky. _____   Once   up - on   a

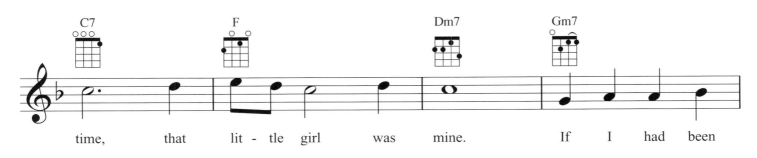

time,   that   lit - tle   girl   was   mine.   If   I   had   been

Up on the Roof

Words and Music by Gerry Goffin and Carole King

First note

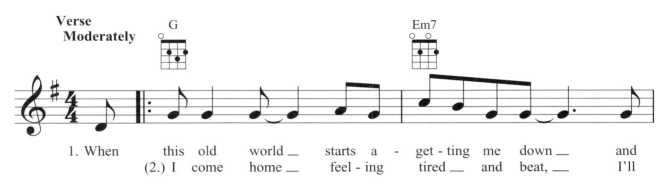

1. When this old world — starts a - get - ting me down — and
(2.) I come home — feel - ing tired — and beat, — I'll

peo - ple are just too much — for me to face, —
go — up where the air — is fresh and sweet. —

I'll climb way up — to the top of the stairs — and
I'll get far a - way — from the hus - tling crowds — and

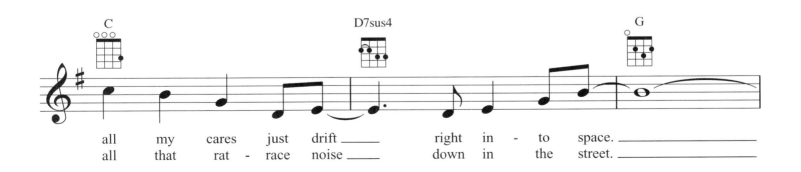

all my cares just drift — right in - to space. —
all that rat - race noise — down in the street. —

On the roof, __ it's peace - ful as can be __

On the roof, __ that's the on - ly place I know __

_____

and there the world __ be - low __

where you just have __ to wish __

1.

___ don't both - er me. _____

___ to make it so. _____

2. So, when

2.

Up on the roof. _____

Interlude

(Instrumental)

Bridge

At night the stars __ put on a show __ for free, __

Uptown

Words and Music by Barry Mann and Cynthia Weil

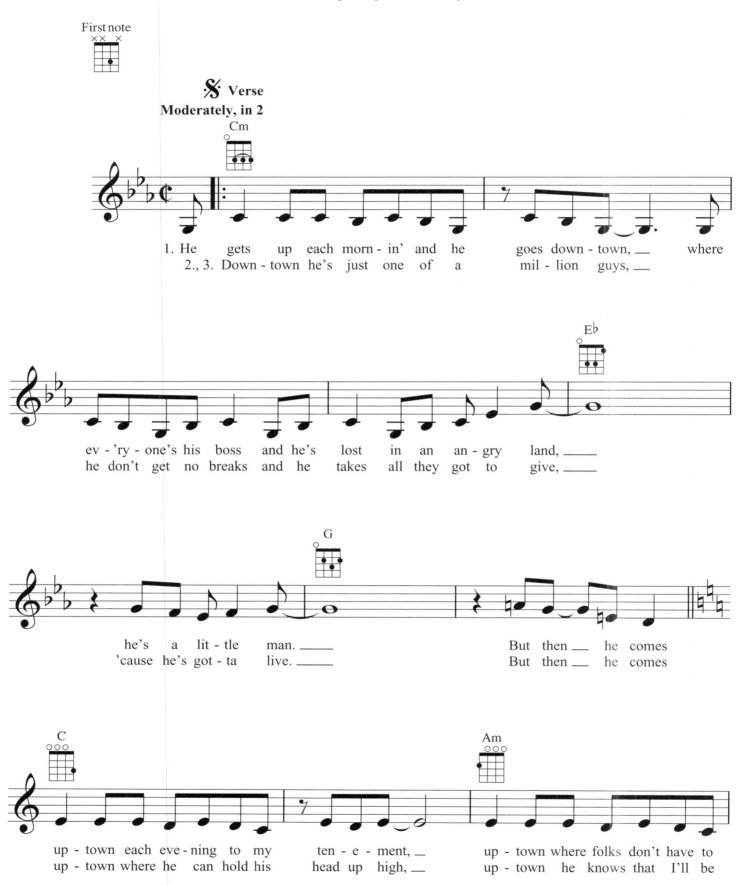

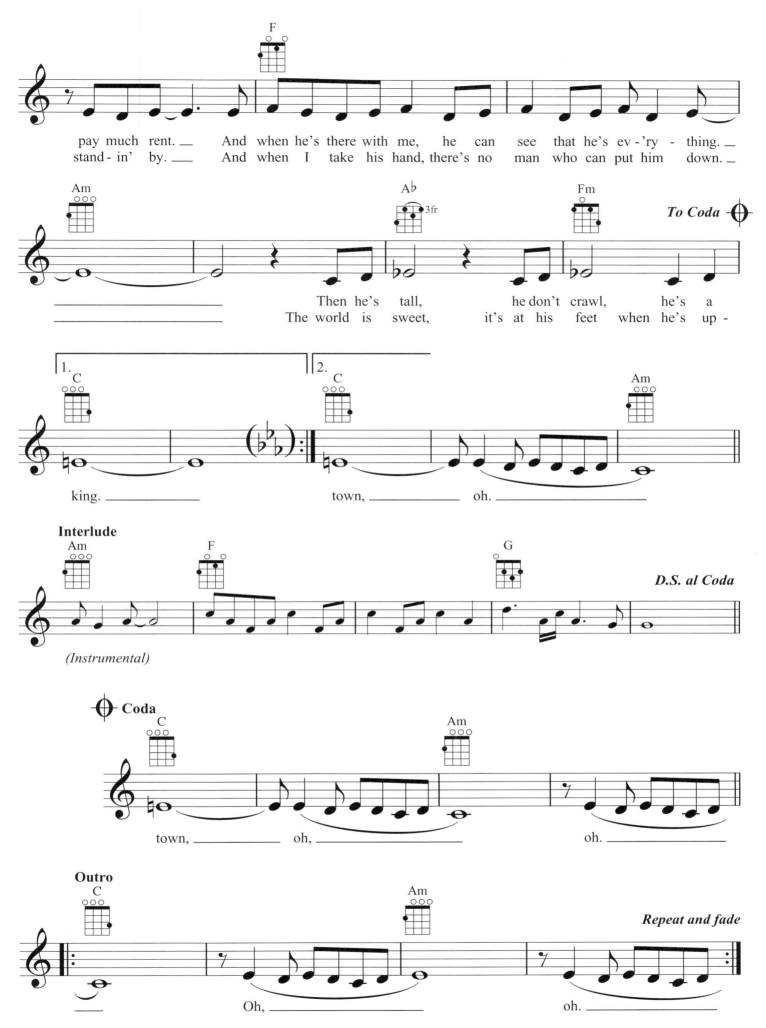

pay much rent. ___   And when he's there with me, he can   see   that he's ev-'ry - thing. ___
stand - in' by. ___   And when I   take his hand, there's no   man who can put him   down. ___

Then he's   tall,   he don't crawl,   he's a
The world is   sweet,   it's at his   feet   when he's up -

1. king. _____

2. town, _____ oh. _____

Interlude

(Instrumental)

D.S. al Coda

Coda

town, _____ oh, _____ oh. _____

Outro

Repeat and fade

___ Oh, _____ oh. _____

Walking in the Rain

Words and Music by Barry Mann, Phil Spector and Cynthia Weil

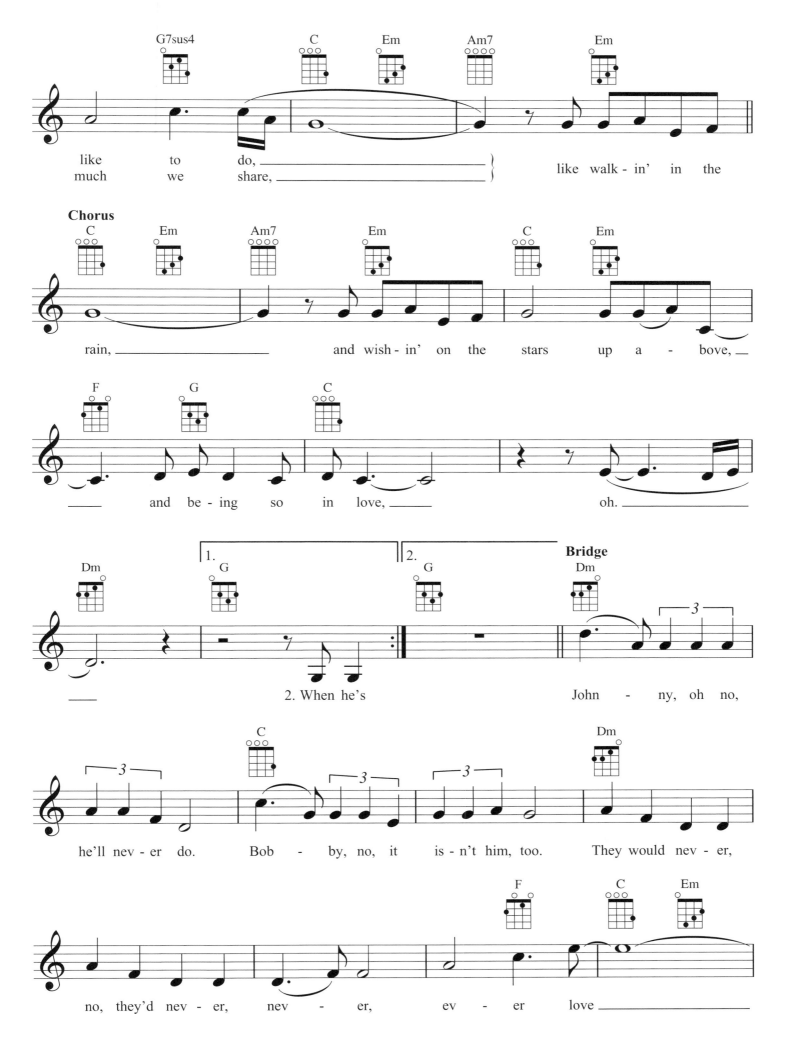

You've Got a Friend

Words and Music by Carole King

Additional Lyrics

2. If the sky above you should turn dark and full of clouds
   And that old North wind should begin to blow,
   Keep your head together and call my name out loud, now.
   Soon I'll be knockin' upon your door.

We Gotta Get Out of This Place

Words and Music by Barry Mann and Cynthia Weil

First note

1. In this dirt - y old part ____ of the cit - y
2. My lit - tle girl, you're so young ____ and ____ pret - ty,
3. See my dad - dy in bed, ____ he's ____ dy - in'.

where the sun re - fuse ____ to shine, ____
and one thing I know is true: ____
You know, his hair is turn - ing gray. ____

peo - ple tell me there ain't ____ no use ____ in tryin'. ____
you'll be dead ____ be - fore ____ your time ____ is due. ____
He's been work - ing and slav - ing his life a - way. ____

1., 2.   3.

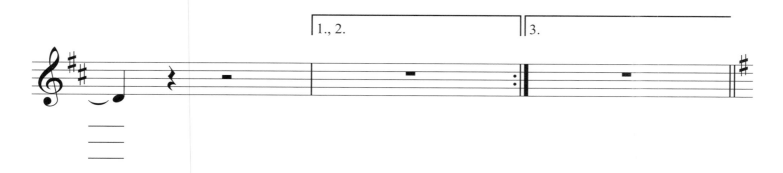

Chorus

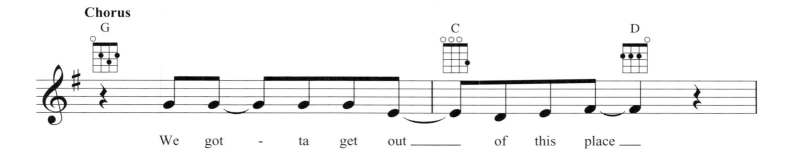

We got - ta get out _____ of this place ___

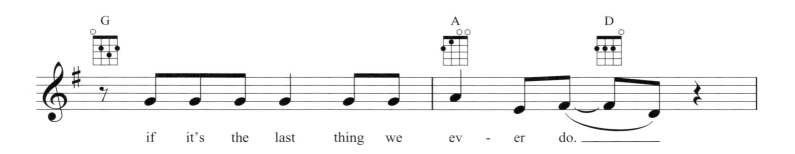

if it's the last thing we ev - er do. _____

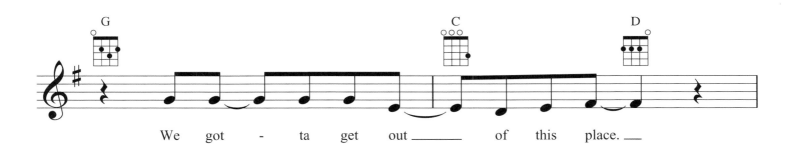

We got - ta get out _____ of this place. ___

Girl, there's a bet - ter life for me and you. _____

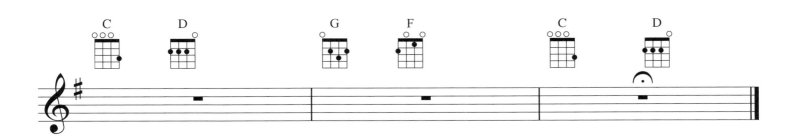

Who Put the Bomp
(In the Bomp Ba Bomp Ba Bomp)

Words and Music by Barry Mann and Gerry Goffin

Will You Love Me Tomorrow

(Will You Still Love Me Tomorrow)

Words and Music by Gerry Goffin and Carole King

You've Lost That Lovin' Feelin'

Words and Music by Barry Mann, Cynthia Weil and Phil Spector

whoa, __ that lov - in' feel - in'. You've lost that

lov - in' feel - in'. Now it's gone, gone, gone, whoa. _____

1.

_____ 2. Now there's no _____

Bridge 1

Ba - by, ba - by, I'd get down on my knees for you _____

if you would on - ly love me _____ like you used to

do. _____ We had a love, a

Bridge 2

love,   a love you don't find ev - 'ry day. _____

So don't,   don't,   don't,   don't let it slip a -

way. _____   Ba - by, ___   (Ba - by,

ba - by,   I beg you please, _____
ba - by, _____   beg you please, _____

please, ___   I need your love, _____   I need your
please, _____   I need your love,

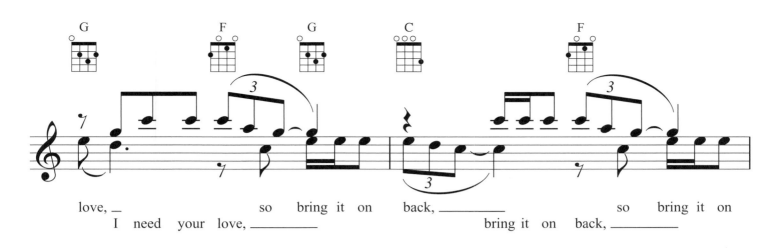

love, _____ so bring it on back, _____ so bring it on
I need your love, _____ bring it on back, _____

Outro-Chorus

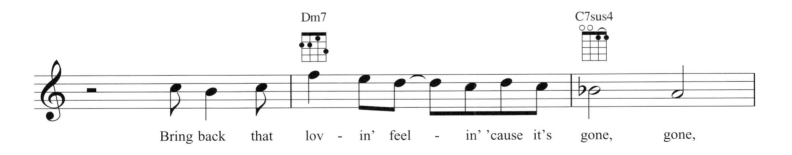

back. _____ Bring back _____ that
bring it on back.) _____

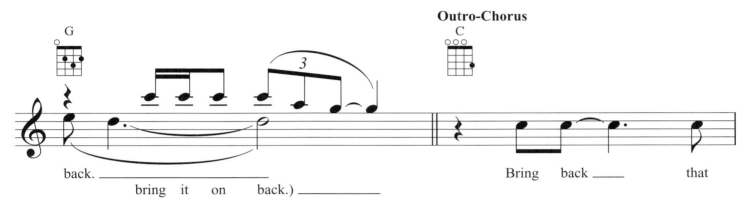

lov - in' feel - in', whoa, _ that lov - in' feel - in'.

Bring back that lov - in' feel - in' 'cause it's gone, gone,

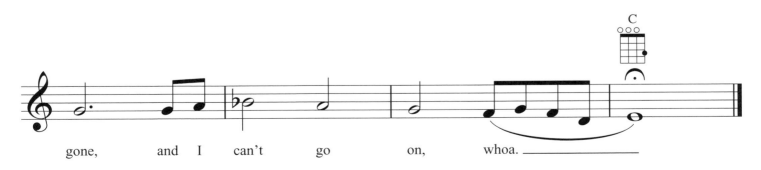

gone, and I can't go on, whoa. _____